Love to Dance

Hip Hop

Angela Royston

Raintree is an imprint of Capstone Global Library
Limited, a company incorporated in England and Wales
having its registered office at 7 Pilgrim Street, London,
EC4V 6LB – Registered company number: 6695582

www.raintreepublishers.co.uk
myorders@raintreepublishers.co.uk.

Text © Capstone Global Library Limited 2013
First published in hardback in 2013
Paperback edition first published in 2014
The moral rights of the proprietor have been asserted.

Edited by Nancy Dickmann, Catherine Veitch,
and Abby Colich
Designed by Cynthia Della-Rovere
Picture research by Elizabeth Alexander
Production by Alison Parsons
Originated by Capstone Global Library Ltd
Printed and bound in China by CTPS

ISBN 978 1 406 24948 4 (hardback)
16 15 14 13 12
10 9 8 7 6 5 4 3 2 1

ISBN 978 1 406 24953 8 (paperback)
17 16 15 14 13
10 9 8 7 6 5 4 3 2 1

British Library Cataloguing in Publication Data
Royston, Angela,
Hip hop. -- (Love to dance)
793.3-dc23
A full catalogue record for this book is available from
the British Library.

Acknowledgements
We would like to thank the following for permission
to reproduce photographs: Alamy pp. 6, 18 (©
AlamyCelebrity), 25 (© Lebrecht Music and Arts
Photo Library); Corbis pp. 7 (© Erik Isakson), 13
(© Imaginechina), 17 (© Mango Productions), 22
(© Heide Benser), 23 (© Ted Soqui), 28 (© Anna
Carnochan/Retna Ltd.), 29 (© Ocean); Getty Images
pp. 8 (Jeff J Mitchell), 9 (Nick Onken/UpperCut
Images), 15 (Phil Dent/Redferns), 16 (Ollie Millington/
Redferns via Getty Images), 20 (Steven Lawton/
FilmMagic), 21 (Dean Treml/Red Bull via Getty
Images), 26 (Trae Patton/NBC/NBCU Photo Bank via
Getty Images), 27 (Patrick Lin/AFP); Rex Features pp.
12 (Globe Photos Inc), 14 (Ray Tang); Shutterstock
title page (© R. Gino Santa Maria), 4 (© chaoss), 5 (©
R. Gino Santa Maria), 10 (© R. Gino Santa Maria),
11 (© Kovalev Sergey), 19 (© R. Gino Santa Maria);
SuperStock p. 24 (© fstop).

Design features reproduced with permission of
Shutterstock (© markrhiggins, © CAN BALCIOGLU,
© Hannamariah, © Paul Clarke).

Cover photograph of a woman dancing hip hop
reproduced with permission of Getty Images (Larysa
Dodz/Vetta).

We would like to thank Allen Desterhaft for his
invaluable help in the preparation of this book.

Contents

Some words are shown in bold, **like this**. You can find out what they mean by looking in the glossary.

This is hip hop!

Hip hop is energetic and exciting. The dancer may start slowly, but soon their whole body is moving with the pounding music. They dip down, balance on one hand, and twist their legs in the air. The crowd cheers.

What's it all about?

Champion hip hop dancer Roxrite says: "The best thing is that you feel free when you're doing it."

Breaking

Hip hop dancing began in the 1970s. A **DJ** called DJ Kool Herc noticed that many kids waited for the musical break during a song before they danced. He looped, or repeated, the breaks to give them longer to dance.

DJ Kool Herc

B-boys and b-girls

DJ Kool Herc called the boys who took up **break dancing** b-boys, and he called the girls b-girls.

Dancing in the street

Hip hop began in the streets of New York, USA. B-boys showed off their moves on street corners, in school playgrounds, parks, and public spaces.

The battle

Hip hop dancers take it in turns to dance. They try to outdo each other's moves. This is called a "**battle**".

Tricky moves: freezes

Freezes are for b-boys and b-girls with strong arms! In the baby freeze, the dancer balances on his hands and head, and brings his legs level with his waist. Then he freezes, or stays still – without falling over!

baby freeze

One-handed freeze

In the one-handed freeze, the dancer balances on just one hand.

Popping and locking

There are many styles of hip hop dancing. **Popping**, **locking**, and **boogaloo** are **funk** styles. They are less acrobatic than **break dancing**. The dancers make jerky moves, like robots, in time to the music.

popper Zhuo Jun

Electric Boogaloos

Boogaloo Sam invented popping and boogaloo.
Sam called his group the "Electric Boogaloos".

Basic move: moonwalking

In moonwalking, dancers look as if they are moving forwards when they are moving backwards. To moonwalk, lift the heel of one foot and slide the other foot back. Then lift that heel and slide the first foot back.

Moonwalking is also called the backslide.

Famous moonwalker

Many dancers began moonwalking after they saw Michael Jackson doing it in his performances.

Dance crews

Hip hop is not just for dancing on your own. A **crew** is a group of dancers who create their own moves. Crews compete against each other in **battles**.

The dance crew Diversity became famous after winning a TV talent show in 2009.

Local friends

A crew is usually a group of friends from the same neighbourhood. They dance together and experiment with new moves.

Hip hop gear

Hip hop dancers wear loose, comfortable clothes, such as baggy tops and tracksuits. B-boys and b-girls like flashy jewellery, trainers, and baseball caps.

Hip hop culture

Hip hop is closely linked to **rap**. Rap became popular when **DJs** began to speak over the musical breaks in songs.

Competitions

Hip hop competitions are where **battles** count. There are different events for solo dancers and for **crews**. Some competitions are local, and others are national.

Bubblegum Crew

Roxrite

The world's best dancers compete at Red Bull BC One and the World Hip Hop Championships. These international competitions take place every year in different cities.

The skills

To be a hip-hop dancer, you need a good ear for rhythm – your dance has to keep time to the music. You also have to be fit and able to move your body in lots of positions. You will need to practise a lot.

New styles

Hip hop dancers keep creating new styles. Krumping, for example, is fast and involves jabs, arm swings, chest pops, and stomping.

Tricky move: the windmill

The windmill is a spectacular and skilful move. It starts with the baby **freeze** (see page 10), but then the dancer spins around with his legs slicing the air. It has to be seen to be believed!

This move is called the windmill, because the dancer's legs whirl, like the sails of a windmill.

Where to see it

You can see hip hop in music videos on television and on the internet. Search online for videos of particular moves and performers. It is even more exciting to see hip hop live, on the street, or in local competitions.

CJ Dippa on *America's Got Talent*

Worldwide

Hip hop is popular in many countries, particularly in the United States, Japan, France, Britain, Australia, and South Korea.

Give it a go!

Everyone can dance hip hop! You don't have to be as good as the best dancers. Join a class, or begin with a DVD and your friends. Get creative and give yourself a cool name.

The result?

You will have lots of fun and become fitter and healthier. Expressing yourself will make you feel more confident.

Glossary

battle contest between hip hop dancers, in which each dancer or group tries to perform more impressive moves

boogaloo style of hip hop dancing usually performed to funk music

break dancing fast, acrobatic dancing, in which different parts of the body – especially the hands, arms, head, back, and hips – touch the ground

crew group of hip hop dancers

DJ short for "disc jockey", a person who spins records and mixes music

freeze move where the dancer freezes in a balance

funk style of music that was popular in the 1970s and 1980s

locking energetic style of dancing, in which the dancer suddenly holds a position for a moment

popping funk and hip hop style of dance, in which the dancer clenches the muscles and then relaxes them so that the body jerks

rap style of music, in which rhyming poetry is spoken over background music

Find out more

Books

Hip-Hop and Urban Dance, Tamsin Fitzgerald
(Heinemann Library, 2008)

Hip Hop Dancing (Snap Books), Joan Freese
(Capstone Press, 2008)

Hip-Hop Dancing, Kathryn Clay (Pebble Plus, 2010)

The Story of Hip-Hop, Melanie J. Cornish (Tick Tock, 2009)

Websites

www.5min.com/Video/How-to-Dance-Hip-Hop-18631033
This video clip shows you how to dance some basic hip hop steps.

www.allworlddance.com/2011/08/2011-world-hip-hop-dance-championship.html
Find out about the World Hip Hop Championships 2011, and watch Bubblegum, from New Zealand, in action.

www.breakinconvention.com/artists/electric-boogaloos-usa
This website tells you how Boogaloo Sam invented popping and boogaloo, plus a video clip of him dancing.

Index